A Collection of

Various American

Holiday Poems

Belinda Sipling

BookLeaf
Publishing

A Collection of Various American Holiday Poems © 2023 Belinda Sipling

Presentation by *BookLeaf Publishing*

Web: www.bookleafpub.com

E-mail: info@bookleafpub.com

ISBN: 9789395969475

First edition 2023

DEDICATION

To All Those Who Celebrate The Holidays

New Year's Day

With a drop of a sphere
The new year is now here
Parties and great happenstance
Are the norm in this circumstance.
Cheers and fireworks are at a full roar
They are determined not to be a bore
There are resolutions galore
Thus, having many goals to adore
People have a chance to refresh
Now that old year is but to cherish
Looking forward is now the trend
There has to be something up ahead
Closer connections, better health,
The only goal cannot be on wealth
Love, family, betterment,
Will lead to a better temperament.
One may not better the upcoming year
However, one can be a dear
And be the one to change this year

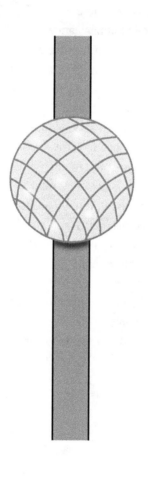

Groundhog Day

What do we have here
A month into the new year?
Where humans ask a rodent
To predict the future
He then turns and greets his
Permanent darkened doppelganger
Will he greet it with joy
Or hurry back within his barrow
Others gather to see the fabled tale
What will the groundhog declare?
He then asks his shadow
What the weather will bring down
The mammal does not spot
His opaque form and goes forth
The crowd cries out in joy
Less winter to come, hooray!

Valentine's Day

Hearts, companionship, and flowers,
What comes to mind at this hour?

Dinners, champagne and wine
Many couple hopes to have an enjoyable time

Embraces, kiss and the like
Are the norm on this romantic night

Rings, smiles, and doves
Celebrate married love

President's Day

In the holiday populated month of
February
There was a future leader born

George Washington of Virgina
Providence
placed on earth that February morn

In the year of 1789
Washington
Was the president prime

He served two terms as
President
The best of all time

After he left the
USA
Had many presidents hence

Not quite the number fifty
America
Has a list of leaders dense

Some good some great
Others
That we could appreciate

However, this day
Washington
Is the one that we can all relate

Since he is after all
Father
Of all our county

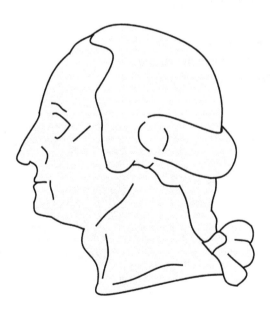

St. Patrick s Day

If your favorite color is green
This is your kind of day!

A man hundreds of years ago
Wanted to tell of Christ to an island long ago

A celebration of the Irish
And the clover green

The unmistakable accents
Unforgettable landscapes
Do not let their memory go

Easter

The day death had lost its sting
Death no longer has victory

The day that the Son of God rose
His grave is now empty

The problem of sin was so great
That Jesus could not wait

To give humankind the chance
To get to right with God Almight

There is nothing more worthy
To celebrate to be clean

Sin does not mark us forevermore
Satan's power is limited even more

The greatest sacrifice ever made
Was made for us all

Forever more, we can be
Grateful when love incarnate
Died and rose to never die again.

April's Fool Day

Want to play jokes?
Want to play tricks?
Want to catch someone off guard?

This is the day for you!

Harmless practical jokes are the name of the game
To make someone laugh

This is the day for you!

Everyone must be willing
to be a good sport
There could much fun to had

This is the day for you!

Jokes, jumps and loud noises
So many choices for
Your future recipient

This is the day for you!

One clever ploy
And you got them
No, April's fools

This is the day for me!

Mother's Day

Today is the day to celebrate
One of the two that made you

There is so much to say about
the one who labored for our existence

She who fed us at all hours
Listened to our cries

She nurtured and gave all
Through our youthful years

She held when the world's pain
Came around our ears

She cheered over deeds
Whether they be large or small

She defended like
The fearsome she bear of old

She remembered the details
Dislikes, dates and fears

She loves us through
Every stage, good or ill

For you see, the greatest title
For women far and near

Is nothing short of
Mother dear

Memorial Day

For patriots of all sizes and ages
Freedom has a bloody wage
Their time, energy, and store
Was spent on battles gore
Their youth & innocence
Gone in the complete sense
Their bodies never whole
Their minds carrying a toll
Their families don't get back
The same man, bloody and cracked
Do not forget the man
who is under a grassy six-foot ban
He died not just for a flag
Or a well written tag
To him, his freedom wasn't first
Yours was the reason for his life's burst

Flag Day

There is a banner
that symbolizes
Our nation of the USA

A day that confirms
the multicolored
Standard's birth

Red to symbolize
Valor, courage and the blood
Shed by those who were

White to show purity
And innocence of its
citizens

Blue to remind us to pursue
Justice as well to keep vigilant.

Then in a field of blue
Fifty stars are gathered
To represent 50 states hewed

So in this month of June
Remember what this flag stands for

And try to emulate what it represents
To bring honor to our beloved Stars and Stripes

Father's Day

Without this half
of this loving duo
We would not be due

Our dear fathers,
They lead without fear
Loving their sons and daughters

On this day let us honor them
Let them be respected
Appreciated and honored

Do not neglect to thank
For all their secret sacrifices
Whether of time or of the bank

They toil and heave
Just for our needs
Without them we would indeed grieve

Authoritative and brave
They set up boundaries
That our souls do crave

Gratitude to the hero
Whose value to us
Will never be zero

Independence Day

Freedom
It had not yet been grasped

Singularity
It was far from being achieved

Hope
Could this actually be done?

Bloodshed
There was much to be called for

Fifty-Six
Men signed and risked

Philadelphia
This document's first home

Great Britain
Its receiver be

Thirteen
Colonies could be made one

Sacrifice
Of eight years and

Two
Centuries and still it goes

Fireworks
From coast to coast

Granted
This independence should never be taken

Labor Day

Summer's end is near
We have worked hard to get to here

School is about to begin
The family must be brought in

Work is closed for the day
Let us feast, hip, hip hooray

Grill is the on the menu
Do not be shy to try the old and the
New

Relax and remember
This chance comes once a year

Patriot Day

A day that has
Changed so many numbers
A nine and an eleven
Three thousand and the number two
The date of the ninth month
And its eleventh day
Just the stating of that day
Sobers everyone who hears
Almost three thousand families
Were divided by death and murder
Family members that will not be
Complete until the afterlife
Two towers that stood tall
were struck down
Two fiery prisons that held
So many last breaths
Those tarnished numbers
Serve as a ghastly reminder
Do not forget evil exists
Or spoiled more numbers will be

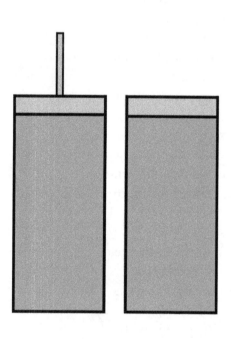

Halloween

Candy, Candy, Candy
What a sweet treat to eat

Party, Party, Party
That will be hard to beat

Costumes, costumes, costumes
They will spark joy or fear

Tricks, tricks, tricks
They will be brought to bear

Pumpkin, pumpkin, pumpkin
They will be a main course

Autumn, Autumn, Autumn
This is where Halloween is found of course

Thanksgiving

This holiday grants us leave
To feast and not to grieve

There is so many blessings
We each have, you see

Firstly, we were born
To be able to see the morn

Our body's wealth
Or alternatively, called our health

Our five senses allow us the pleasure
To partake of life, most sure

Our experiences, each one of them
Makes us unique and not dumb

Our relatives and friends bare
Their hearts with tender care

Finally, thank our God alive
for in Him we truly thrive

Christmas Eve

A month has gone by
Since the holiday last

The night before the
Most popular holiday

In between these two days
Preparation is in store

The presents are laid to rest
Wrapped in their paper best

Warm cookies and milk
Are left for elves or those of their ilk.

Stockings are filled to the brim
Their receivers will not be grim

When all is done
The preparers had to their rest

Knowing that all is left
To celebrate and give to all they hold dear

Christmas Day

Tumultuous morning
Excited shouting
Hurried steps
Impatient offspring
Longsuffering parents

Multicolored scraps
New belongings
Wishes Granted
Joyful shrieks
Smiling relations

Holiday music
Clanging silverware
Chairs scrapping
Dinner aromas
Familial chatter

Cold temperatures
Warm beverages
Sugary treats
Musical cheer
Cozy warmth

Warm bellies
Heartfelt goodbyes
Sleepy eyes
New Memories
Christmas Love

New Year's Eve

It is nearly here
The brand new year

All we have is till midnight
Then we get to say good night!

Bubbly beverages galore
Spheres begin their downward tour

Calendars are made anew
What could the next year brew?

Recollections and resolutions
Are now the subjects of conversations

The countdown has begun
The old year is almost done!